# paint

# draw

# color

# cut

# glue

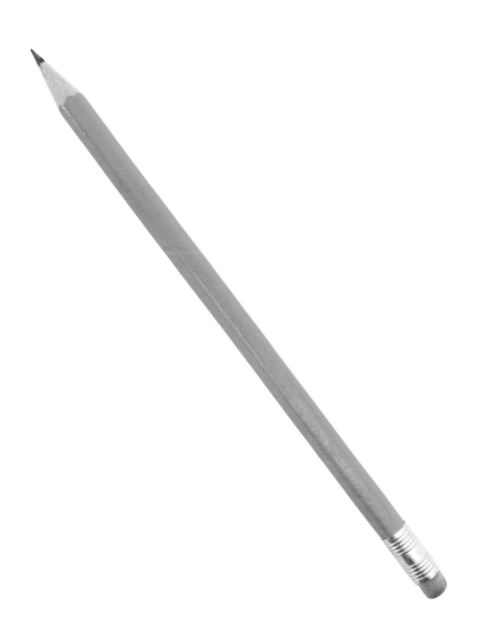

# pencil

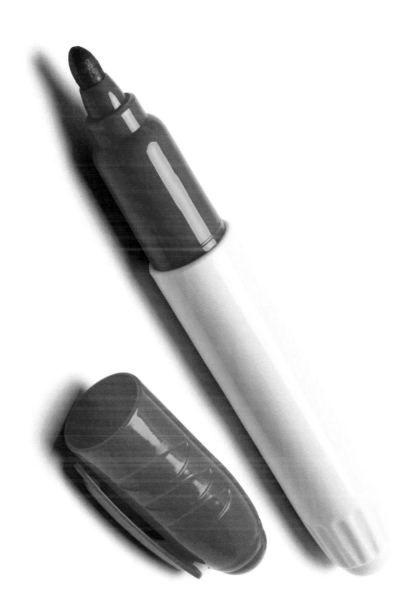

# marker

# paintbrush

# glue stick

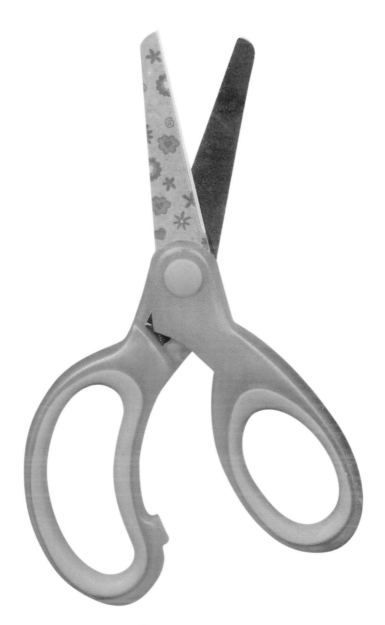

# scissors

     Cambridge Little Steps Level 2

# brush

# toothbrush

# towel

# soap

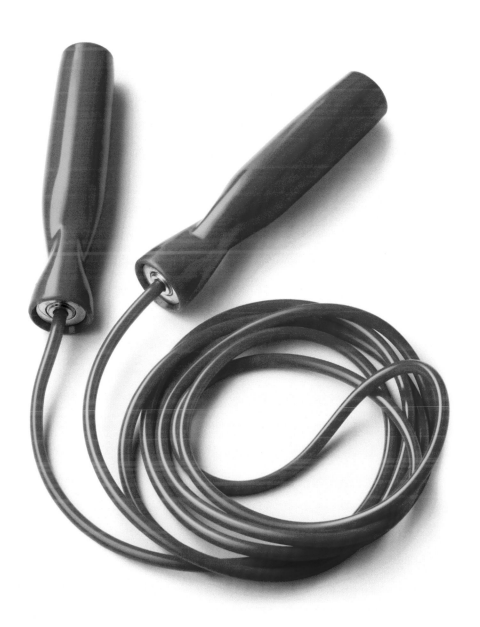

# jump rope

# thirsty

                                   Cambridge Little Steps Level 2

# tired

# dirty

# hungry

# sick

# living room

# dining room

# kitchen

# bedroom

# bathroom

# shower

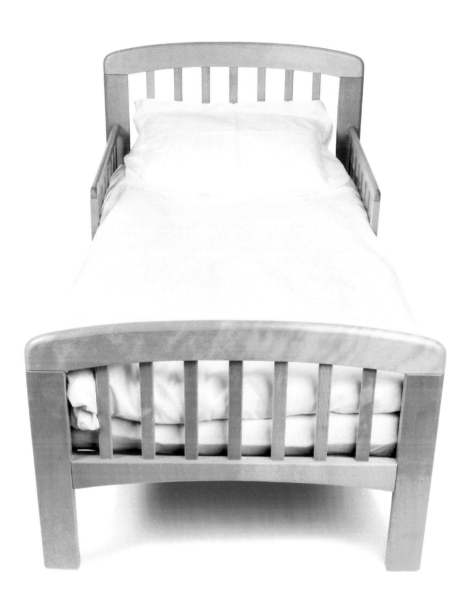

# bed

# couch

# lamp

# fridge

# COW

# hen

# duck

# horse

# sheep

# calf

# duckling

# lamb

# chick

# foal

# eggs

# chicken

# salad

# rice

# pancakes

                    Cambridge Little Steps Level 2

# soup

# orange juice

# cereal

# fish

# strawberries

# milk

# water

# pants

# shoes

# T-shirt

# sweater

# socks

# jacket

# boots

# raincoat

# dress

# skirt

  Cambridge Little Steps Level 2

# sunny

# snowy

# cloudy

# rainy

# windy

# soft

**7.1** Cambridge Little Steps Level 2

# rough

# smooth

# good

# bad

# sweet

# salty

# loud

# quiet

# beautiful

# car

# train

# bus

# airplane

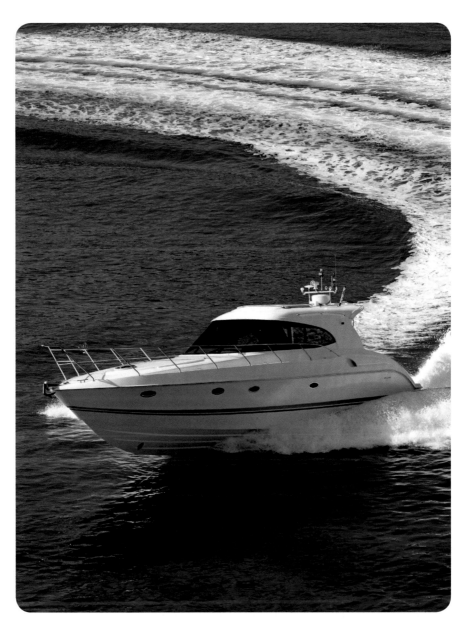

# boat

# bike

# helicopter

# ship

# beach

# city

# amusement park

 Cambridge Little Steps Level 2

# mountains

# seeds

# shovel

# hole

# water

# dig

# watering can

# petals

# stem

# leaves

# roots

# Leo, Mia, Tickles